excerpts from

carol lee sanchez

excerpts from A Mountain Climber's Handbook

(selected poems, 1971-1984)

by Carol Lee Sanchez

Taurean Horn Press/Out West Limited

Some poems in this book have previously appeared in *Beloit Poetry Journal*, *Backward Dancer*, on a Strawberry Press broadside, *Message Bringer Woman* and *Time Warps*.

ISBN: 0-931552-06-0
Front Cover Design: Carol Lee Sanchez
Front & Back Cover Layout & Back Cover Design: Gary Whitney

Introduction

I

. . . and they presume
to tell me
-i- must build my FREEways
with perceivable stuff
limited to their range
of perception

and i say:
catch me if you can

Yes. Let this be a warning to you: your range of perception may be in danger. Smoke may come out of your ears . . . Brave it. This woman of color, a phrase which is applicable in every conceivable sense of the terms that compose it, does build freeways. The first book of poems by Carol Lee Sanchez I had the pleasure of publishing, *Message Bringer Woman*, the title being the English translation of Carol Lee's given Laguna Pueblo name, starts out being a personable account of growing up in twentieth century America as "a mixed breed" and, as the reader moves through it, magically transforms itself into a paean to celebrate her own unique identity (& by example, to celebrate everyone else's as well.) This happens because the poems don't just say it, they sing from the timeless place. I won't presume to be able to "catch her" or tell you how she makes them do that. But I will try in this introduction to tell you what I have learned in my twelve year association with her poetry.

This is the offspring of the forementioned book. All the poems come from a much larger work, *The Creation Myth of Message Bringer Woman*. Instead of focussing on the rainbow songs as the earlier work did, in *excerpts from* ***A Mountain Climber's Handbook***, the focus becomes poet as prism (with the light shining through). Don't get me wrong, the rainbow songs are, of course, here & they are still very important, but this book has been arranged so that we are constantly jarred into coming to terms with the many in the one who wrote this book as well. (For a partial list, see Afterword.) How does this happen? Most poets cultivate one distinct voice in which to be recognized as they create the world/poem as they comprehend/sense it. This helps with the identification process which, not incidently, helps sell books. Carol Lee Sanchez, as you may have been able to gather from my prejudiced point of view, is not most poets. She challenges the reader not to be lulled into believing they can completely understand the world the poet creates for them because part of that world is hers alone. With lines like:

you give my mask to me
and ask me to see beyond
my fantasy of self.
you enter the doors of my body and mind

to find the shape of your hope
your love   your pain
to find the   no beginning
with no end.

these are not comfortable poems. They examine many of our core beliefs & they look at them from a variety of perspectives—all personal to Carol Lee. There is very little "ivory tower" here. Each poem comes from/is the poet creating herself. Because of this they are personal for us too and engage our involvement. They become, as she called her first book, multi-dimensional "conversations."

II

> I am a Mestiza. A crossbreed. The product of four distinct cultures and customs, five different languages, three different religious influences, though I was primarily raised and trained in one, the Catholic Faith . . . Much of this background shows up in my poetry. I have described it for myself as: the immediate emotional experience of the Arabic/Latino influence/layer; the reflective careful and particular word choices and rhythms of the Indian influence/layer and the objective intellectual distance, sometimes abstractness of the Anglo influence/layer. In my mind I resemble a pousse café . . . in short, American, from my points of view.[1]

Carol Lee confesses to three influence/layers. Perhaps you can call these influence/layers: voices? I would say maybe in their purest form you might, but this "mixed breed" is seldom in pure form. There's too many atoms in her composition that boast of historical perspectives & not all from an identifiable material plane of existence. Instead I'd like to scrap the idea of voice (for this intro to Carol Lee Sanchez' poetry) & offer these influence/layers to you as lenses through which her light passes. *excerpts from* ***A Mountain Climber's Handbook*** is a showcase of these lenses. Take the following examples:

a) the old ones crowd the edges
of my consciousness
think me   thoughts of fragmentation
stare me through and
all around me ask me to articulate myself
through them

b) Joker ridin high
whirl me madly
into earthly atoms
flesh of my flesh
thought of my thought
created out of myself

c) the work is going well. wires hum with
intricate communications   reaching
proper destinations. impedance levels
below tolerance   all clear for the next
issue of communiques . . .

The first has careful, medium length lines. The second has short rhythmic lines and the third has prosaic, abstract lines with apparently arbitrary line breaks. Can you find a voice familiar to all three? But, isolated, as they appear here, they can be recognized as descriptive of the same process seen through different lenses. However, hidden within their separate texts & part of another "whole" context, the poem, there is something so radically different about them, especially thematically & rhythmically, that though they *may* be related, their likenesses probably would not be recognized unless they were looked for. This is one of the poet's techniques I call her layering process. These "accidental similarities" act cumulatively as knots in a mesh that force us to see, perhaps on a subconscious level in most cases, the world from different viewpoints—simulataneously. Now do not interpret this as saying that Carol Lee Sanchez writes the same poem in different ways. Exactly the opposite. As you read these poems you will notice that after these "meetings," each poem goes on its own way toward a completely different end. This simultaneous vision evokes the experience of depth.

III

To understand how this happens, my simile of poet as prism can & should be taken literally: Carol Lee is also a painter:

my colors unfold my symbols,
sandstone mountain edges northern horizons.
in Quincy   there is sandstone
and on my house altar.

She paints with oils and with ideas. Her word choices & juxtapositions create density. The kind that unfolds with re-reading. In the above passage from "the road to Blue Mountain," sandstone, as I read it, becomes a color and a quality of the mountain; while in the third line it becomes an object which is common to a geographical area & sacred for her. The word "sandstone" has been opened up to define the perimeters of a particular experience of "north" for the poet &, in its being expressed, for us. This is the unfolding process. She continues:

Yellow Mountain Woman/*moe a na ko ko ote*
carries my vision, holds it in keeping.
sa ma ka mo kaits/daughter of the lion
lioness cub she   dreams true
speaks for: Yellow Mountain Woman.

What did I say earlier about feeling uncomfortable? Do not feel shy if this is a strange tongue for you. (It is the Laguna dialect of the Keresan tongue—she also uses Spanish and Arabic in her poems.) You may feel dumb. I do. I think that is a common experience among non-Keresan-speaking peoples. Even in Chinatown. Carol Lee is reader-friendly. She cares enough to give clues for the unknowing. I believe her use of the slash "/" designates an appositive relationship between multi-lingual phrases. Thus, Yellow Mountain Woman, a.k.a., *moe a na ko ko ote*, carries her vision. It is my guess that Yellow Mountain Woman is perhaps another symbol for the sandstone mountain in the first strophe, one that unfolds further meaning. For one, the mountain has become a woman, daughter of the lion, a sandstone-colored animal, who dreams & speaks for herself. & so the poem & the colors unfold.

I could go on & may when I have closed here. I hope I have given you some ideas about why I think Carol Lee Sanchez is an innovator in the realm of poetry. I think just the casual reading of these poems will bring pleasure without any need for my theoretical observations. But for those of you who like this sort of thing, I do indeed hope I have served my purpose.

Bill Vartnaw
San Francisco, 1985

DEDICATION

I lovingly dedicate this third volume of my poetry to Bill Vartnaw, creator of Taurean Horn Press, for his years of friendship, constant encouragement and active belief in my poetry. Although academically trained in the western Euro-American literary tradition and a fine poet in his own right, as an editor and publisher, he has never judged what I had to say or how I have said it on the page. Because of his unique ability to see beyond his own cultural biases and socialized preferences, he has embraced the many different voices and cultural view points that find their way into my poems, never demanding that I find one consistent voice, be culturally pure, sexually explicit, academically acceptable or politically correct in accordance with literary fashions of this time. I gratefully acknowledge the time and energy he has spent selecting and arranging this volume of poems as well as the investment of his own resources to bring these songs to you - my readers.

TABLE OF CONTENTS

introduction ... iii
from crystal ... 1
song of the four winds ... 2
the old ones ... 3
creation story ... 6
flint stories ... 9
sun chant cycle ... 10
the dream of crystal woman ... 13
emergence stories
(for my lebneni ji-do ... 15
(for the atseye's & gunn's ... 16
(for my father ... 17
(reclamation ... 19
(allá en el rancho gallito ... 20
(for my mother-july 1977 ... 22
the road to blue mountain ... 25
laguna daughter: journey ... 26
flint stories ... 34
'he thought to expel blackness' ... 35
for the cloud people ... 37
morning prayer ... 38
silver woman's songs ... 39
notes from black elk ... 40
this is my body ... 42
the two worlds of the red nations ... 44
the vision of eagle ... 46
flint stories ... 48
old spider's stories ... 49
(rain ... 53
from silver mountain ... 54
words are like singing they say (to lorca ... 56
words are like singing they say (to olson ... 57
corn children ... 58
cowgirls and poets ... 61
blue lake song ... 62
coral woman's song ... 64

squash blossoms 66
vision: prophecy: ceremony 68
afterword: the universe as artist 70

from crystal

whole bread and milk become meals
sprinkled with clarity and mirth.

what is this sudden need to share the superb
dance of bubbles, whalespouts, rain forests and deserts?
cells and splendor should not combine to
grow such fire between us.

a bass horn and a thrush begin the night here.
i have dreamed your name and heard a
fragment of your song.

there is a tear
hidden in a faraway thought-
a night once dreamed and disappeared.
what futures do we initiate or compromise?
which self occupies these moments we converge our
histories into a common memory?
-is this immortality then?

i chose cobalt skies to carry my reflections,
roses with thorns as life and music and love.
this future/present
already marked in my past.
i was not looking for this connection
between   -this now
when i dreamed you   as you are.

song of the four winds

to inspire a careful language
cautious for other centuries-
we summon
these portfolios out of ourselves.

around us
the halls are crowded with name tags
immortalized in
gold leaf and celluloid
everywhere.

we-
document the quiet change,
the particle dispersement of:
a particular level of thought.

we-
walk the edge of the unknown
planting specks of light to note
our discoveries.

the most useable path through oblivion
will bear the mark of:
the careful explorers
we've become.

we-
will continue to prosper here,
unnoticed for awhile until:
all the webs are untangled

and they will find us__
holding the ends of these threads,
a smile caught between us.

the old ones

1.

the old ones make patterns
just outside my perception;
external blueprints move to appear
from beyond visibility.
i cannot unfocus enough
to refocus on the message
i need to hear.

my life crammed with:
bits of lives
scraps of ideals
pieces of change
that belong to fragmented visions:
not my own.

it is the killing of things-   that bothers.
the separation of: this from that
the analytical shattering of:
countless living things.

the old ones crowd the edges
of my consciousness
think me   -thoughts of fragmentation
stare me through and
all around me.   ask me to articulate myself
through them-
the once was order and conversation
that they knew and shared with
all living things.

2.

these certain people
argue life.

distribute anger onto unknown forces
isolate and separate to:

find a cause
that wrought effects
that cut them down.

the whole
escapes the point of focus
the balance- held inherent in all that is
and i fall back
fall
outside the thoughts the old ones bring
become again those:
bits of lives
scraps of ideals
pieces of change

fall back into analytical shattering of:
living things.

3.

those feathers come
to guide my path
encourage my heart to understand.
the old ones come to speak
in many ways:

be strong
(they say
be good to yourself
(they say
be careful for yourself
and the life
you share.

and they say:
you must learn to observe everything
so you will know and understand your own power,
the power of your own way.

you should learn these things: carefully
if you are not careful: you will hurt yourself.

the old ones come
appear at the edges of my vision
remind me to care for myself -and
the *words* i discover
                                                            for:
                                                            (they say
                                                            words
                                                            are like singing.

words   are like singing
                                                            (they say.

creation story

joker ridin high
whirl me madly
into earthly atoms
flesh of my flesh
thought of my thought
created out of myself
remember the taste
of oceans lapping beach
sand semen salt
upon my lips.
those magic days of
hangin loose
and wanderin life
on carousels
with nickels and dimes
in cut glass dishes
and the kewpie doll
from the valentino lover
just off the boat from italy.

dejavu got us all-
hooked us on our
wildest dreams
mocked it up in
living color
added sound, taste
smell and touch.
i want to hallucinate
a hundred new realities
a wild night just ridin high
my windy hair runnin free
warmin up by firelight
a hundred more imaginings
to talk about
and then goodbye
and off again.

sometimes i sense
the heat of you

the question held
behind your eyes-
                    mangos dipped in goats milk
                    harem veils, *derbukke* beats
                    know the ages i have walked.

i want to run away with you
a magic moment on my tongue
then run from you
to disappear to where
you cannot find me.
you imagine the taste
of foreign in the
tingle of your skin
                    platanos frying, *frijoles negritos*
                    marimbas singing palm trees
                    into hot *acapulco* nights

un pecado del alma
take my body
mi corazón
one magic moment
between my thighs
and then goodbye
and off again.

i have this thing-
this fascination for *gueros*
a weakness of the flesh
for *ojos azules*
'blue eyes':
                    that intoxicate my reason
                    that hammer in my blood
                    that destroy my equilibrium
                    that coerce me into dreams

like the one who gave herself
to 'yellow hair' and betrayed
the dark eyes of her people
a million memories ago.
i understand the insanity
of her treason
and   his.

i understand the fire
in your loins
the hair rising on
the back of your neck

wanting to know and explore
the mystery of darkness
mis ojos negros
siempre negros:

> holding secrets of wailing walls
> and *müeddins*
> *la llorona* and *tenatzín*
> *si its che na ako* and cedar smoke

luminous layers of
earthly illusions.

joker ridin high
whirl me madly
flesh of my flesh
thought of my thought
created out of myself
pecado de mi alma
take my body
mi corazón.

flint stories

hurry!   hurry!   hurry!

fasten your seatbelts, adjust your goggles
and be prepared to submerge. the descent
is long, but quick, unless you resist the
gravitational pull. resistance will cause
a shock that can short circuit an entire
network, fusing all recorded imagery into
overlapping fuzzy renditions of what was.
the vortex of the whirlpool is relatively
calm. deadly quiet as in the eye of a
hurricane.
in between the edge and the eye -the
holocaust abides (to bend and shape
or break the whole. to scatter the bits
into anonymity of -never was.

no mark   no place
no name   no face

the work is going well. wires hum with
intricate communications -reaching
proper destinations. impedance levels
below tolerance -all clear for the next
issue of communiqués.

-the speed of thought is squared yesterday;
the day before you wind back up in yourself-
she capsuled with capable ease.

sun chant cycle 1)

she:) wanted to remain a spy
undisturbed in her passivity
or   a confirmed marxist with
no new creed   to expound.

the crisp edge of this hallucination
cut through tongue-thick-wobbly words.
she:) told herself   the difference was
doing or not doing   the stuff
they called   their life.

anything and everything is bought and sold here
and it's so easy   and so hard   all at once.

                    rome. paris. london.
mexico city. tokyo. hong kong.
centuries reconstituting levels
reflections of duplications   the deviations
only slight variations   of every theme
that ever was.

trace the vintage of any line:
each word's transition through any age discloses
truth   or humor   or deceit
and many times
the lack of vision   beyond that day.

sun chant cycle 2)

she:) inhabited her universe tenaciously
holding on to the crevices and
tiny bits of obsidian singlemindedly.
days froze in unison   and sometimes
slid past each other with no marks
or scratches for identification.

occasionally her memory coincided with a
particular day and a forgotten friend
came to call.
the visits began with a specific intent;
gossip to share
out of date events to
re-examine and put away with several
cups of coffee and half a pack of cigarettes.

the conclusions she reached heralded a
new combination of possibilities to activate.

the friend always carried a personal message
to her
unaware most of the time that they did that-
but she knew.

and the messages she sent herself
moved her into other dreams.

sun chant cycle 3)

she:) dreamed of other lives and places
covered over with
sacrificial moratoriums
sacramental paraphernalia   and
felt drowned each awakening.

the choice is always adamant
no matter how carefully considered   so
she pulled the ballot box from the rack to
make her thoughtful x's
in each appropriate box
as she pushed notable fragments

through her mind.

she:) assumed a different   posture
momentarily;
her mind resolved to
note some long forgotten medicinal recipes:

> boil pine needles to get tar
> or   place a stick in a pine tree
> no.   that was too wasteful
> and cruel.
>
> sassafras tea!
> lots of sassafras
> a general tonic
> good for everything.

the dream of crystal woman

masks crumble and disintegrate
long before the legend that wears them melts away.
papier-mâché dragons see their predestined slayers
with comic accuracy.
the fool is the perfect cipher;
zi-pher   the aleph   no beginning   no end.
two half moons unite into an integer named: one

you call me to you to lie down beside you
remove my clothes to leave my body
naked and trembling
stripped of manner and make-up
no cover for my mortal fear.

what faces have you ripped away
to disclose what hides beneath?
what yesterdays lie stacked in your attic costume trunk
that can wear tomorrow with less terror
and more understanding?
we seek only the mirror of ourselves in others.
what self will we seek if we shatter or
blacken all the mirrors in the land?

you give my mask to me
and ask me to see beyond
my fantasy of self.
you enter the doors of my body and
mind to find the shape of
your hope
your love
your pain
to find   the no beginning
with   no end.

man is born of woman on this plane
from womb to heart
through mind and eye

returns to suckle at her breast
to feed again and again.

returns to the peaceful dark of her caves from battle
to hide in warmth,   to be healed and made whole.

this reality is hidden among subtle games
separated into masters and puppets
neither certain whose strings they hold
whose image they duplicate.
master and puppet must have each other
through all the worlds at large.
must take turns as: master puppet   puppet master
to walk tomorrows into mirrors of terror
and dreamless sleeps.

do you see that without your seed
i am barren and will wither into
winter's night of frozen cold?

do you see that you bring life into me
as you enter my doors
keeping death's scythe at bay?

do you see that we hold
the thread of life between us
so carefully drawn from seed and womb
spun into delicate balance?

you call me to you from my secret knowing
and as i become you,   you become me to know:

that man is born of woman on this plane
from womb to heart
through mind and eye

suckles at her breast and leaves
to return again   and again
to sustain   the no beginning
with   no end.

emergence stories

(for my lebneni ji-do

this grey edge of winter falls: subdued.   demure.
keef helek, ji-de.
i did not understand my tears in a market
street movie house;   tears not shed
that winter beside your grave *lebneni ji-do.*
your stake in america - decays in seboyeta;

("not fair, hija . . .
worked to lose what your father built—
in depression times.

("change ebry-ting, estos carajos!
jóvenes!

grey rain this day.   no snow.
no cold hard winters here.   no barns.   no stables.
no orchards here   lebneni grandfather.
no big land   hard to work and hard to ride.
("all gone, hija . . . dose days

i hear you again, transposed to a movie screen
lodged on this fog shrouded thumbnail peninsula
("no saben nada. . .
your voice fades into trolley bell traffic outside.

("I go myself.   ma-má.   ma-má
big city noise like new york seen with your
little boy's eyes.   you used to tell us
about *ru-me*, in the cedars of lebanon.
i don't know them with my eyes, only peach
blossoms in my city backyard,   coating concrete;
spring message of new patterns.   growing.

aousalem aoulaikem ji-de Nasíf.
your dreams fulfilled.   everything changes.
salud pioneer grandfather.
lebneni merchant.
land baron   and   lawmaker.
salud   y   adiós.

emergence stories

(for the atseye's & gunn's

great grandmother was indian.
born on the reservation
educated at carlisle
married to a whiteman
scots/irish -from ohio.

great grandfather came west with the railroad.
he was a surveyor then. he fell in love
with a pueblo girl and the wild new land he found
so he stayed in the territory and
became a part of its history.
he made a fortune
(in sheep and cattle
and lost it.
he made another-
and left it.

and from the union of meta atseye
(oak clan/laguna pueblo
and kenneth colin campbell gunn
gunn clan/harding county ohio
the issue was seven: four daughters and three sons.

of the Bar 15 ranch- there remains only the
record of title once held in valencia county-
giving the usual descriptive dimensions.

it also remains in the memory of those
who are left
who lived near or were raised there.

grandma was raised
on the Bar 15.

emergence stories

(for my father

you were the middle east   and my father.
old country   and new
come together at the end of an era;
a young *patrón sin hacienda*
y rancho grande   to oversee.

just this side of   two worlds clashing,
you walked along the borders-
saw new ways, forms and fashions
come into being.

you were old country   the head of the house
the father i worshiped and feared
as a girl;
the man who could solve any problem
remove all obstacles;

you were the man of the house
not to be sassed   nor disobeyed
not to be upset   nor disturbed.
merchant by profession-
up early, gone to work;
community leader by choice-
gone to meetings, home late.

you were the echo of europe   and my father
the stern voiced command
the last word
the father who taught me
horses, cattle and sheep
who taught me   the store business

a romantic idealist
walking the line between two worlds
clashing.
first generation   -born in america-
you were old country when your father's
empire crumbled around you

and while still a teen-ager
determined to build "anew"
from the ruins of the old,
left "wild hell-raiser" and "rich man's son"
behind
and became america   growing up.
you were america;
son of an immigrant pioneer
from lebanon
son-in-law of an immigrant pioneer
from germany
successful small town american
business man, community leader,
controversial state official
and my father.

now retired from politics
retired from the store business
you are still dedicated
to the freedoms
and rights guaranteed by
the constitutions of your native state
and this "great nation" of the Americas.

now   a senior citizen,
you again watch new ways, forms and fashions
come into being;
still   the man of the house
(not always the last word
you remember other days of
two worlds clashing.

you are america   and my father.
your honesty
your uncompromising faith in
participatory democracy
your belief in "the rights of the people"
and your romantic idealism
i take from you
as my own-
to pass on to future generations.

emergence stories

(reclamation

great grandmother: it all went with you.
those sacred dances and
how to understand them.

i don't know the measure of the meaning they held
or the right way
to sing them.

you left only a part of your blood and heritage:
a few stories and
three bracelets for
me to keep.

the spirit of you is strong in me
and i gather up those
traditions
though i lack the
practise of them.

(allá en el rancho gallito

my mentors could not be considered: dudes.
gentleman ranchers they were
those texan/mexican/indian cowboys
who gave me my code of honor.

taught me a lot of things about
bein and doin

ridin herd/round-up time
ropin/brandin/markin/loadin
shipping cattle

i watched them and learned as they worked:

diggin post holes/droppin posts
stringin wire/ridin fence
pitchin hay/ridin bronc
gettin thrown/climbin back up
stayin on

i waited for a quiet sign:

an almost wink/a passin smile
a quick nod/a gripped handshake

those cowboys taught me their way of bein
and doin.

they lived as they said
did as they thought
offered no quarter
contained what they knew
struggled with "progress"
stayed where they were -and
died as they'd lived.

my mentors could not be considered: dudes.
they were a strange breed of men:

"not to be found this side of hell"
-they'd say
"in a world gone soft on pride
and honor."

gentleman ranchers
they were.

emergence stories

(for my mother - july 1977

a week before st. anne's, i closed my eyes to sleep
and saw your face in perfect detail.   startled, i
thought you ill until i saw your smile.   then i knew
you were at quiet worry   -checking on your babies.
each one.   turning bits of conversation back and
forth in crossword-puzzle fashion   with quiet remorse
in radio soft   'wish you could do something/make
it go away'   sleepless nights.

santana's day again.
sixty-one earth rounds and the years seem long
and separate.
we chose different paths   you and i.
two women,   each doing what she thought best, neither
approving nor disapproving of the other   -openly.

you: good wife/mother/grandmother/perfect
homemaker. still caring for the man you love-
married at sixteen.
i: wife/mother/artist/scandalous/rebellious one
leaving a string of husbands and homes behind;
would not follow in my mother's footsteps
nor have her example   -be mine.
rebellious i: determined to have equal privilege
in this   'man's world'   of america   (the land my
immigrant grandfathers loved
i: would be recognized!   me: a woman!
beyond acceptable roles of: housewife drudge/typist/
clerk/or schoolmarm.   no perservering
storybook heroine,   i!

and who can know the why of it?
the determination/conflict of wills/lifestyles?
and finally-   the silence.
the stretched silence between us.
how cruel we youngly are,   demanding life
with righteous fury!

we forge our spirits in different fires you and i.
i: enduring what i thought was pity, pushing out,
ignoring heartache, leaving safety behind while you
thought: 'poor her/poor children/she's really had it
hard' . . . no. i made it hard
to temper my scattered inclinations/perfect my arts/cope
with a creative drive that drove me to destruction—
a drive larger than wife and mother could hold.

i made it hard; i needed discipline to maintain/no
matter what/no letting go/no breaking the hold.
(no whispering grandmother's likeness -here.
i made it hard. because i had to. and i was proud.

2.

you tested me each step of the way.
'are you sure/are you happy/well if that's what you want/
i worry about . . . .'
your mother concerns leap unbidden.

these emotions we struggle with well up inside us
move muscle and tissue into knots wrap our bones in
weariness. this issue we call: motherhood- that
all mothers perceive with different eyes and women in
their womanhood not quite able to share these
honest differences because some other pattern was
handed us as: our example.
now i: the rebellious one, who would not give way
reflect on the choices we've made as i
welcome my forty-fourth year.

you: who laid aside your pen locked inside you
your stories and verse and read someone else's
to your children
you: who gave up the soft touch piano for busy wife
and mother (but kept your books and records close
you: who might have sat at mary austin's feet-
hauled water/bore babies/changed diapers/scrubbed
floors/baked bread simply because you loved him
in that 'either-or' world that was raised in you.
'that's the choice i made' you'd say

and   ahh good woman
you stuck by it   all these years.

lady: woman whose womb once held me close
mother: if i take nothing else of you-
                    i take your courage: to keep.

the road to blue mountain

my colors unfold my symbols,
sandstone mountain edges northern horizons.
in quincy   -there is sandstone
and on my house altar.

yellow mountain woman/*moe a na ko   ko ote*
carries my vision, holds it in keeping.
sa ma ka mo kaits/daughter of the lion
lioness cub she   dreams true
speaks for: yellow mountain woman.

from the long dream
he carried thunder sticks from north wind
reminders of cold spots still left
in mother earth.

yellow songs melt ice and snow.
gold rays from *o srahts*/father sun, permeate
bring me closer to blue mountain.
i know what is to be.

from fabled *cibola*
wa puh/west, i came in search of honey
beyond the place of the snake people/
shru wi ha no
beyond the island of
hard beings thought woman/*si its che na ako*
to the edge of the great water
kow aish o   puts
to find this vision first dreamed on
sandstone hills   in childhood.

northwest of   *shipop*
lies rainbow bridge
northwest of   *shipop*
lies golden gate bridge.

from *cibola* i came to   blue mountain
to find this vision whispered once by
yellow mountain woman.

laguna daughter: journey

extend the ligament and bend the arm of the old man
it furthers one.
it is the myth that is important.
these myths recreated: impacted crocodiles and
razor blades.

my icons are disturbed. vague.
they are distilled in the depths of primal mists and must
not be moved until they are ready.

i begin my journey to water.
i meet 'mother-machine' and confide my distress.
i tell her of my dreamscapes. ask her to tell me
what she knows. she does not reply.
i find a beach with undisturbed sand. there is
no one there. i decide to write my letters in that place.
when i am finished i will know the meanings of
my icons and where i have hidden them.

dear mother machine: i went to witness
an artistic male birth. golden calves leapt from
his throat. a new primitive, like 'dallas' talked about;
strangled in sumeria. or maybe babylon. he
reappears in carnivorous forms waiting.
he waits to mine diamonds baking in his gullet.
waits impatiently. digging too soon discloses
carbon dust. a powdery substance not worth
the cost of failure. back to babylon to rediscover
the dead spaniard artist's motif and maybe
reinvent the gutenberg. who knows
what century 25 holds for him.
the diamonds may be cooked by then.

my icons cannot be seen through
those microscopes. will not disclose evidence
so obvious in four dimensions. only five eyes
can comprehend the final form.

dear pinball: she tried to
cook rubies in her fingernails. tempered, tapered,
plunged deeply into muscle and sinew.
scraping bones for content and didn't notice
that rhinestones and glitter were all she found.
i watched her hair scream day and night
for relief. for sustenance.
wailing strands strip eucalyptus trees
trying to remember cudzu clawing elms and oaks
to pieces. the gold tooth hangs from the
ceiling catching lamplight on certain days
and squanders radiance past the window glass.

dear janie: my vulnerability is
not the source- each cell discards itself
separately falling ever so slowly
caught up in imperceptive acrobatics throughout descent.
nova blossoms scatter pollen into cracked brains
holding skulls together to keep out worms.
the careless scratch did not know it had begun
an aerial display.

the insides of any nightmare must
contain more than this. wakeup! wakeup!
one more spiderweb will get loose but who
will it catch? and what for?

dear bob cat: it's the voices i can't describe that
tend to stick in corners and unfinished elevator
shafts. i keep wondering who began the
imitations so rampant around here. did they just
divide and divide away from the original cell? or
beget and beget each other - exchanging
protoplasm with every division of: echos leaking
through sponges, broken toilets
and plastic flower pots? suppose a new wooden leg
fumbled with a foam rubber tit
in the parking lot at lover's point-
what symbols could be catalogued from such
an event? what great myths could be culled,

transcribed and studied at great length?
would you identify with the wooden leg?
or the foam rubber tit?

dear northwind: there are
these archetypal visions and symbols and
substance banging around in the atmosphere
and no matter how fast i run
or where i hide they will find me. **will**

locate me and proceed to label themselves
upon all parts of my being. what then i ask?

some noted translator will come up to me and
begin to explain the labels- and the reason for
the fixation of them on the various parts of my body
and why the translator knows more about it
than i do! **and** if you dream beware!
you may alter a universe you were just getting used to
and have to begin again to find out where you are-
all because of those damn echoes.
sonics distend the faculties of perception-
cloud mirrors and break glass and mango seeds
if you're not careful.

dear yellow woman: i found
a starter in the middle of the junkpile last week.
i was saved from hallucinations and costly pretense.
starters are rare items. the rarest substance
on earth whereas: duplicators are
everywhere. under sidewalks. inside tunnels.
posing as grocery stores and factories. in steam
engines. jet engines. lead type. ink bottles.
beside trash cans. floating with soap bubbles
and even hooked to helium balloons and computer
tapes. but the holy of holies the starter
holds the sacred rites of renewal, regeneration
and transcendence beyond the complex to the complete.
the starter can be duplicated without end.
the duplicated can divide and echo

without end. they cannot start- cannot
regenerate- cannot begin again from
nowhere out of nothing.
only starters are equipped to begin.

i am following all these threads to make sure my
icons are holding up. so many things to look for.
i really need to be sure. how can i
punctuate the arbitrary definition of a rule? it's
probably best to puncture it and watch it
subside gracefully.

dear jim: i would
like to ask you a lot of questions- but i'm afraid you'll
turn out to be a myth. i mean- it could happen
what with you being a poem persona. do you read
labels? those damned echoes again.
voices sliding together. cicadas rubbing legs.
garnets growing out of mica schist storing plasma
in crystals just in case. i expect it will be
some time before you answer. it's okay. i can wait
for answers. sort of like waiting for my
icons to appear outside the marble casements where i
hide them. waiting can be good sometimes.
especially if you're not ready for questions.
p.s. i hope your repeater is inked and running
well and your writer/operator is keeping you
greased and oiled.

dear ancient chinese inventor:
my eyes are stained with other visions not mine.
sincerity and science fiction plot well timed
mechanisms. some confusions send parts
and pieces outside the reality i originated. some
hairy teeth invade my awareness and i pause
to place that image in some related
context. i fail.
grasshoppers protest the habits
of bees. not everyone can sift nocturnal
silos for true nourishment. mold creeps

quickly into everything.   the racial memory of
wasps   could prohibit honey and   even
beeswax   if they should breed with bees.   the
seeking continues.   i climb the faces
of cliffs   touching   what i know.

dear kraut: i still can't find my icons
and symbols.   did i leave them in your pittsburg
ovens?   or possibly in your slag heaps?
beehives? anthills?   bees and ants would do
well to associate with each other.   their
societies tend to have similar structures   are
notably matriarchal   and   have **queens!**
our queens-   old dragon finder   *pretend*   to
thrones and devise legendary robes, mythic
crowns   and carry sceptres filled with carbon dust.
uncooked sceptres that pretend to rule:
grasshoppers and wasps.   i think my
confusion stems from weights and measures.
turquoise leaps brilliant and blue from my
fingers. contains fragments of my song.
even sandstone plays melodies for me i am unable
to translate into sensible language-
and i cannot get through diapers in somebody's else's
dreams   or the spider horrors in   another
nightmare not mine.

a layer of fine scum
overlays most windows i look into   these days.
i'm the only woman i know   who never made it
on inverted propositions and purist theoretical
mumbojumbo.   those subtle decoys disappeared
before i had a chance to use them properly.   i
mean-   the gentle ruse worked: back then
but i was busy being 'good times and up front'!

ocotillo blossoms flame the desert
now. more of my song breaking free.   those: 'candles
of the lord'   filter music through cactus spines
and call don juan   to play kick the can   with
us.   later- we can discuss the possibilities of my

undiscovered symbols in his realm.   until then,
i leave you your pet dragon   resting in your left palm.
this business of nativities will take some time
to unravel.

(beethoven had a part in this-
carrying on like he did while sitting in the ear of his
planetary daughter,   giving her earaches-
tuning her in   on his reality.   i learn to
listen to my own sounds.   she tells me not to go
deaf-   listening.   my sounds. discrete units
of meaning-   adding up to my self creation.   **my**
reinstatement.   molecule by molecule.   medusa
grows flowers   watered in the night-   can
melt pillars of stone with cedar smoke.   can hold
semen and daisies on the tongue at the same time.
-and not recoil).

dear sassafras: that ancient chinese
inventor   told me about inventing indians   and
after eight generations of 'slanty eyes'
would   **de**mand his creation myth   from the
california sierras.   buried four by fours and
rusty spikes hold his bloody legends.   **his**
emergence place is from the bowels of those
mountains   -on the backs of iron rails
ridden by iron horses.   **his** coming out place
lies there   as surely as the 'kraut's' place lies
in the carbon pits   of coaltown.

how can i ask you to be sister without
knowing about those things and places you come from?
yet: our legends must derive from the
same source-   somewhere.   is it possible
to become   from these fragments we so diligently
piece together in song nights and dancing suns?

what oklahoma memory will you find   that can bind
us in tradition so different from those drums
we both carry in our blood?   my bedouin ancestors
must carry traces of your ancestor songs within them.

my blues come from a different source. american
ancestors. invaded. defeated. christianized.
raped. enslaved. murdered by the spaniard.
the sustained note of a coyote howl on a clear
cold night. the slow beat of a solitary drum
at dawn. the steady rhythm of belled dancers
feet whispering in and out of morning winds
across an almost empty plaza.

my blues. filled with lava beds.
sandstone cliffs. sparrows and crows.
barbed wire fences and scrub cedars. mountain
and desert grow inside me. i share them with
you -along with the adobe home of my childhood.

dear northwind: i want to hear those other
songs not my own -and- i've decided it's okay for
me not to be a **'fullblood'** of anything. i don't
have to hide from myself. it's like the ancient
chinese inventor said when he claimed his place of
emergence. **i can** find my hidden icons.

dear ephanie: i have
learned the many new ways and found
some new songs to stir my soul. sometimes
i hear music from other places and i hide. i want to
make my own music. my own myths and legends.
i listen to her 'dangerous music' and it talks to me.
makes me want to sing those mica chips
and crystals to sparrows. there are many
colored women's hands clappin out other rhythms
in her 'colored girls' songs . . . . . .
i can move with them.
through them.

rainbow god and
many-colored corn maiden sit behind
my eyes. they hold hands. come into
this reality. whisper again: the meaning of
my name. remind me where to seek.

how to find shipop again. remember
my place of emergence. kawaik is: my home.
is where i come out from.

i speak my body: *hah-pah-nyi.*
oak. paguate. *qisch- chi.* my first home.
tse-waht-eh-yeh. message bringer woman.

my symbols speak clearly. wind brushes
sandstone. releases my icons.
i too am laguna woman.
i too make 'talking leaves'.

it isn't the function of a square, or the orbital
speed of any object set aloft (he sd.
it's the arc of the path, times the distance of the projected
target area that discloses the selectable range of
possibilities of any given transaction. the margin of
error is minimal and the computation in logical sequence
of this range -will describe the most reasonable
probability. this defines the precise behavior
pattern and the specific series of decisions in numerical
order necessary to achieve maximum return on any
investment including: electronic, atomic, molecular
and elemental.

i:) rescind the battle seemingly enjoined. i have come
only to burn this pile of crisp new green bills -the
smoke of which will send chills of excitement and loss
coursing through your being.
i:) will make you forget all your troubles and understand
my concept of powerful intrigue! (he sd.

> "These are the ravens of my soul
> Sloping above the lonely field,
> Cawing, cawing.
> I have released them now,
> And sent them wavering down the sky,
> Learning the slow witchery of the wind
> And crying on the farthest fences of the world."
>
> (from *The Residual Years* by William Everson)

he thought to expel blackness
from his soul, out into the
atmosphere away from him.
he did not seem to know that
raven is brother to coyote, brother
to spider and badger and crow.
white-skinned, white robed,
he could not penetrate those mysteries
in pure isolation.
raven is more than trickster – shape shifting.

when days change
nights become rivers of memories for
crows and ravens to soar freely
between mind and matter.
he sd.)   it's all in the mind.
a lot of indian nonsense you shouldn't hear.
(from man to raven or wolf and back to man again.
only in the mind.

our sacred beginnings and connections are
lost in your towering skyscrapers;
built from unbaked thoughts on top of
ancestor mounds.   but:
it's all in the mind-   (he sd.
another white-skin rides high on disconnected
uninformed laughter and applause
playing with coyote; mounts coyote's foolish
aspects as theatre   in disregard of his
wisdom and cunning.
beyond his birthright   white-skin explores histories
not his own   and seeks to instruct
those who do not know
in what he does not truly understand.

and even now-	coyote has changed among you,
because of you	shape shifted,
become you-
become more coyote than before.

we should remember that that *c'ko'yo* magic
is still there
working at the bottom of things
and *tsüsh ki* will have the last laugh
along with *ko yem si, ko shar e, ko ko mish* and
kuñ e tyea appearing to be foolish
before the crowd.

coyote doesn't always wear his skin
when he's around.

for the cloud people

we go forth and call the earth
into being.
father sky and rainmaker
ride summer winds
across blue mountain-
speak sacred names
to cloud people;
watch dancers
offer corn flesh
beneath them.

shíwana, shíwana
corn mother thirsts

shíwana, shíwana
dust devils rage

shíwana, shíwana
hide *o srahts'* face

shíwana, shíwana
fill grandmother's breast

keep rainbow god
behind blue mountain
til after you come
then he may bless this village,
these fields we planted.
shíwana
rumble
climb down those clouds
to these mesas below you.
shíwana, come to us:
grandmother waits
corn mother waits
four-leggeds wait
two-leggeds wait
everything waits
we all await you.
shíwana, come to us.
shíwana, come.

morning prayer

to the east:
            where grandfather lives

to the north:
            where cold comes from

to the south:
            where warm winds blow

to the west:
            where grandmother earth has her place

i offer my song.

ask clarity for my confusion
ask purity for my heart
that i may know my purpose
my harmonious place in the order of things.

silver woman's songs

(for dorinda moreno

a   la   roooo
         roooo
         roooo

from the heart
corazón de la tierra -untamed land
defiant still-
you sing your grandmother's lullaby
and the *yei* of her people come
to give strength to your song

a   la   roooo
         roooo
         roooo

          from a hogan
to an *adobe casita*
she lost the ways of the *di ne*
the people we call: navajo.

mestiza
you walk proud
carry the *grita* of *chicana* women
on your lips
and the song of your grandmother
in your heart.

a   la   roooo
         roooo
         roooo

            the *yei*
of your ancestors
smile on you.

notes from black elk

(for wallace black elk

-carry this song breath sacred to grandfather
offered to four wind directions -like that
those commitments answered and there you
are   living it.
one of those sundays   inside this long life day
and there's no headlines, only a few whispers, someone
sneaking out-no patience for 'broken-english indian
stories.'   no headlines that say: **black elk speaks!**

standing on this sacred altar   -like that   he prays in
lakota.   **black elk speaks:** we got to reconstruct. get
together. all of us. reconstruct that philosophy before
everything is destroyed. -that philosphy of the *true*
cross - the four wind direction cross - before that other
cross coupled with a gun came and damaged the balance.
-that balance maintained for a long time by 'dumb
indians'. no bureaus of ecologies then   -because
grandfather, *wakan tanka*/sacred spirit taught them
respect for all living things on our sacred altar; for this
planet we ride - our grandmother earth.
-sacred things must be used with respect. then all is
harmony among the four-leggeds, two-leggeds,
wing-people, snake-people, many-legs people. everything
belongs to grandfather.

wakan- **black elk speaks:** through grandson wallace,
here in a california university, to help the new
beginning. -we must reconstruct the philosophy that we
have damaged- all together; red people/yellow people/
black people/white people. try to think as the other
thinks. communicate through the spirit. never mind the
languages here in this university of universities.
on this sacred altar, we will come together   -like that
with grandfather to open our minds, our hearts
and help us to work together. otherwise the sacred fire
we play with will destroy us all.

no headlines for simple words. for broken english. for lakota holy man granted the sacred power of vision. no headlines for coming together in unity of effort and spirit. only the cross of condemnation and crucifixion screams across front pages.

the cross - still coupled with a gun. peace backed with bullets. **black elk speaks:** describes the song of the four-wind directions. tells us how to communicate with grandfather:

wakan
stick stone
feather bone
tobacco sage

wakan
fire earth
air water

wakan
these symbols
of life
these gifts from
grandfather.

wakan/sacred
and we must
share with
each other.

this is my body

this is my body
to have and to hold-
to infect, pollute, humiliate
wound, cleanse, contaminate
addict -or not.

this is my body
to have and to hold-
to fatten, reduce, girdle,
show off, hide, pamper
batter -or deny.

this is my hair.
to cut, to dye, to streak
to bleach, to kink, to straighten
to grow as i please.

this is my face.
to stain, to powder, to paint
my nose, my eyes, my lips,
my ears, my cheeks, my chin
to scrub, oil, cream, pluck, pierce & shave
to remove wrinkles and pouches from
or leave to weather and age.

these are my breasts.
to give and to take away
to nourish my babies by giving
to feed my vanity by not giving.
to uplift or let sag
to enlarge or remove
they belong to no one -but me.

this is my body
to have and to hold-
my temple, my domain
to do with as i will
to inhabit or cast aside
if i so choose.

my body, my temple, my domain
not ever to be ordered or disposed of
by church or state
without my knowledge
without my consent.

no black robed justice or judge
no white robed pontiff or priest
can claim legal or moral right
in true conscience
to dictate the use of my body
by me.

you: fathers, brothers and sons
who unjustly legislate
the use of my womb
then hide behind the *law*
to subjugate my body
to your will and desire-
threaten my life
every minute of
every day
in the name of your male god
and the preservation of life.

you: righteous rapists, exploiters
and murderers
accuse me   of your crimes!
this is my body
my temple
my domain.

you: mothers, sisters and daughters
who virtuously agree
to give up your bodies
to church and state
beware the sons you birth!
where will you turn
when they bring *you* to trial?

this is my body to have and to hold
to do with as i will.

the two worlds of the red nations

'For those who live/ in the two worlds:
There are so few of us, let us/ be good
to/ one another.'

(from Southline by Gogisgi/Carroll Arnett)

-there's no such thing as indians
in north america-
that professor sd. to me.
-not like they were, they're
all gone, you know-

(sun dance pole/sweat house pit
four corners marked and colored true
above, below and middle place
corn mother dances green today)

i paused to think what he might mean
and he continued on:
-now panama has *real* ones, still *wild*
and *primitive*, not contaminated yet-

(white deer dance/bear dance/eagle dance songs
whale blow/raven step and seal feast
wind spirit whistles/koshare clowns)

-i've spent three summers there- he sd.
-to study them. they're pure.
up here, well, they're americans
like the rest of us; no pure
culture to be found-

(morning star and mountain ways/stomp dance
circle dance/northern and southern style, clock
and counter clock/up river salmon ceremony
root digging songs/*yei-bei-che huuhuuhuu*
shalako blessing)

-they dress and drive and eat fast food, the same
as us. oh—there's remnant bits of this and that,
a few folks speak their native tongue-

(blue jeans/cowboy shirts/ten gallon hats
fry bread/navajo tacos/corn-venison-mutton-stew
lambing-shearing-sheep camp time/strawberry festival)

-but all in all, that's not enough to say
there's any indian culture left
in north america-   he sd.

(basket, rainbow, corn and butterfly maidens
acorn mash and corn meal grinding songs
cowboy boots and ribbon shirts/piñon harvest)

five centuries drop quiet here
moving bones through super highways
stories sifted from obsidian bits
pottery shards and willow reeds.

five centuries fall away unnoticed
spring plant to harvest to hunt to
silent winter sleep.
long-time stories still live around here
sweet sage, tobacco, cedar and corn pollen
still offered around here.
old time spirit-talk and medicine songs
still sung around here.

five centuries now, we walked in two worlds-
weaving new stories on baskets and blankets
adding ribbons, beads and bright colored threads
to things we use and wear. work copper, gold,
silver, nickel and brass in indian fashion.

five centuries living and dying unnoticed.
five centuries walking silent and hidden.
five centuries in-between 'the two worlds.'

the vision of eagle

coastal winds whip salt marks onto sand
dash against sentinel rocks scarred with years
of water wounds.
i sit my soul on a wind-braided pine;
a solitary cliff hanger you shared with me
to shed eucalyptus tears that match the sea
they fall into.

i ride the crest of a wave
engulfed in the rythmic current of cycles
re-live the hurting ecstacy of birth
wide/awake/watching as blood flows from my womb.
immersed in the violence of my uterine contractions
the waves: roll/roar/ripple through my body.
an infant skull bone bangs on my cervical gate
wanting release: rips and tears an entrance into growth
not knowing we must both share the pain of
modification through the narrow constricting
tunnel of emergence.

i will contain the nerve shattered cry
that leaps to my throat.
the pain does not matter.   the pain recedes
as quickly as it comes and leaves a new magic in its place.
the sea subsides into gentle caresses,
carries me into visions and dreams.

hope reaches me in the dream.
olympus and fuji remain starkly etched into sky
and legend- no heavenly inhabitants left.
cherry blossoms shower petal tears for the delicate
izanami, water thick needle carpets from bonsai pines
still sculpt and pruned as izanagi directed
centuries ago.
popocatapetl and ixtauhuatl smolder silently
mute testament to what might have been

the dream carries the scent of roses.
you reach for one, encounter a thorn and

become wounded with winter's frosted pain.
i must contain the cry that leaps to my throat.

i will encase one drop of that blood   in crystal;
build a shrine at the summit of a fair mountain
and plant a rose bush   as guardian
to wonder that such fragrant beauty bears thorns
and wounds us to free the giant within.
the pain does not matter.

i walk in a nameless wilderness,
call up a wild i do not understand
along with a longing that crowds my body with
the ghosts of faces left outside me.

who calls me woman?
and turns away because my mind is as productive
as my womb.
all my children are the fruits of both mind and womb.

who calls me friend?
with open hand and waits to receive
whatever gift i have to share.
each deserves no more than giving derives.

who calls me prophet?
wishing only to hear what will benefit and praise.
all the ledgers of the realm hold accurate accounts.
the pain does not matter.
it is a sacred thing to participate
in the act of birth   just as
salt water drops from waves along a deserted beach
fill me with the sadness of knowing.

hope comes in the dream that carries roses
protected with thorns,
eagle circles high, carries my vision for keeping
and i enter myself silently
to wait for
eons to pass.

they walk. two by three. forward into a never
ending curve of complexities. the consequence
of survival has to be surmounted first. after that,
they can proceed into the interim harmony of
stabilized mechanics. pre-empting thought patterns
was not permitted in the first stages. nor was open
warfare. however, controlled quarrelling was
encouraged periodically as a safety mechanism and
as a preparation for advanced, massive encounters.
confusion reigns mostly, intermittently laced with
short periods of order where everyone knows what
they are doing and can barely withstand the shock.
our heroes crowd into phone booths and render
simple communications meaningless within the
time allotments granted; hold daily meetings to
confuse organizations, who in turn, crank out
endless streams of paper into the hands of an
admiring public. our heroines hide in glacine
bags, dispersing **natural** products, committed to
the ideal slogan: 'natural is beautiful' -if you can
just get past the skin of it. the great director in
the sky teaches a seagull how to fly, and the usual
cast of characters are just the usual cast of characters.

old spider's stories

1)

ariadne weaves
delicate patterns.
her looms
hold transparent threads
life colored scenarios
interwoven with time.

doomed to spin forever
the grids of space:

internal monuments
geodesic webbed
globes, suspended
in orbit, doomed
to spin
forever.

ariadne weaves
the grids of space:

time falls gently
from her looms.

old spider's stories

(for fuad

2)

ask for a day.
any day filled with weather reports of
highs and lows and mundane things.

how high do we place any moment of meeting?
the veil is thick between us.
i did not recognize
but only loved you.
so helpless in earth bindings
are we who struggle for light to
move outward into everything.

one moment held carelessly   yet left
behind etched with shock
no one able to understand the choice you made
during your last early morning earth sleep.

ask for a day
in another light beneath a different sun
that we may meet without mist to blind us
and speak softly of earth bound years
once shared.

3)

coeur d'angeline from alabaster shavings
left in powder puffs
those luminescent shadows to hide eyes behind.

remember the orange rinds in her purse
if you intend an incantation.
            the scent will stay your hand
            remake your will and remind you
not to tamper with   witching ways.

attar of roses
oil of myrrh
spinning tops and assemblages of
worried nights.   that man did not
pay attention-
pretended he did not hear orange rinds
whisper dusky in moonlight shadow dances
echoed on distant walls.

            santa teresa,
            rosas del cielo en tus manos.
            who calls this voice
            from mists beyond?

            teresa called her lord (the christ
            to wound her hands and feet
            to bind her soul forever to him.

blood rose petals
keepsake of his promise
floated round her   scented/fragrant
she was sainted.

            heed then, that special burning
            that magic conquered love
            held sacred
            held close in the heart of woman.

ripened mangos burst sweet
flow outward from this mystery
through orange rinds
luminescent shadows and musky nights.

(rain

windows bathed in moisture glitter opaque brightness
and play rainbows on my eyes.

(where do you sit when you think of me?

i walk through thistles to find you on dark nights
listen close to hear you -a breathless laugh away.
i have sung the rain into my soul and danced the cobwebs
into pearls strung round the skull above me.

(what do you hear when a meadowlark
sings?

brambles and thistles pierce butterflies wings
flying blinded into candle light at the center
of an eyeless head -grinning.
the merry-go-round goes spinning inside me
calliope cacaphony jangles my own sound.

(what do you see when the sun wakes you
each morning?

fog brews bubble and burst around me. lower to
soften the eyes of my hardened vision. i can smell
the wet adobe now -rain lashed earthen home
filled with the length of tears.

(how do you speak when you know the
melody of a star?

an ocean will rise to lay waste the desert. make
fertile the desert. make ready for what is to come.
life lives in water along with the gift of abundance.

(what do you know when someone says:
i love you?

shatter the water jar. leave only the shards of
knowledge behind. we will plant them for harvest in
the year of our leaving.

from silver mountain

it isn't possible to remain
in cloister, forever.
(the solidity of
the subject escaped him
along with the identity
factor.

name me
the nameless faces.
call the rolls of lost
unfortunates forward.
relieve them of their
death masks.
reactivate their voice boxes
instead and let us hear
what they have dreamed in
forgotten places of unknown form.
peel the surfaces from
unshed tear drops
one by one
and reveal their
separate crystalled
salts to me.

uncover the coffins
of future's obsolescence
that we may begin to reclaim
our ancestral rituals and so
in reverence -honor our dead.
those ghosts of fantasy
(on television screens
ride across my vision in
nightly panorama of
ancient splendor.

call out to remind me that
what lives once, lives forever-
(as energy released
into universe can never

decrease.   -remains
printed   in the
forward stream of time.

words are like singing they say . . .

(to lorca

lorca-
in castellana
i have prayed to the
spirit of your pen.

to create a god of
this or that
humans will do for some
reason no one comprehends

and i
speak up to you-
not as a god
only that you were so large
so filled with everything.

pained for the least
angered by the thick
hurt by so much because you
did not know your light
was so blinding.

words are like singing they say . . .

(to olson

the master walks on the other side
(a curtain of light between us

across acres of fields for his magic breath
to breathe upon.

no mourning for his quiet rest
no cascade of words across frequencies
to light years beyond.

days continue
move forward
carve extensions of unknown form into
lasting monuments-
more dialogue because our destinies dictate this.

we must remember to breathe
(with each stroke of the pen

to infuse the whole with the light
he left behind.

corn children

(for wendy rose

we gather our bones from many places, look for
familiar marks to determine our identities.
we share the same land marks. places. buildings.
local folks.   seen with different eyes:
        simon,   leslie,   paula,   and i.

i speak mostly of earth with brush and paint.
desert.   mesa.   hill and mountain.   rock.
sagebrush.   yucca and cedar.   thunders
and cloud people.
                                        earth colors
                                        sky colors
hand and eye proclaim on canvas and paper these
visions in my head.   in my heart.

with my brush i describe earth mother-
to remind my children the land is sacred.
this sacred altar that holds the length of one
star's breath.

with my pen i speak of relationships.
with words and the ordering of them, tell little
stories.   keep hold of that harmony i am
part of.   that order of things reflected in being
                                                and spirit.

it seems proper that language should reflect harmony:
                                                a giving way
                                                a moving out
                                                a coming in.

these things we speak about from memory
(as corn children,
these traditions we keep not knowing why sometimes
or how we know the right ways.

many corn grandmothers watch over us
and whisper into the wind to remind us of our duties:

> -you should never take more than you need.
> if you need some reeds for the new whisk broom
> then you go down to the river and tell the spirits
> all around you there, that you
> have come for some reeds.
> you must ask them for permission and
> then you must thank them for providing
> for you.

in this way, we keep in balance.   in this way we keep
in harmony.   we should always be courteous to
everything-   that's what grandma used to say.

bones of thoughts are in those burial mounds or are
around them. sometimes they are disturbed when the
mounds are plundered   but those thoughts remain
for us if we respect our ancestors.
thoughts that come to tell us:
that's the way it is
that's the way it is to be done.

spirit corn mothers watch over us. remind us to
remember.   send their thoughts to us:

> you must respect everything that is here.
> your family, your elders, the animals,
> birds, fish,   -even the rocks and bugs.
> grass, trees, sun, sky and clouds.
> you must remember these stories we tell you.

we tell ourselves to remember.
simon.   leslie.   paula.   wendy.   and i.
that we must respect everything put here.   to restore
harmony.   to restore balance.

we gather our bones from many places. examine them.
mark them.   number them.   sometimes they
speak to us.   speak through us. become words and
pictures to pass on like the echo of grandma's words:

-you should leave one bite of food on your
plate and offer it to the spirits.   that way
you will always have enough to eat.
you must remember your ancestors so they
will remember you-

cowgirls and poets

(for joy harjo

she rode horses on the edge
of dawn
climbed limestone cliffs into
another place
                    of her creation.
images of other times
flowed from her tongue
into the echoes of ancient songs.

somewhere on a windy desert
a silent monument stands waiting
holds memories of wild horses
                    stilled in stone.
another concrete reference point
for rainbows to crowd round
covered with emeralds
garnet dust and
                    eagle down.

6/84

blue lake song

these mornings,   i awake
ask favors of myself.

my eyelids blink sunlit cement into
sandstone razor blades at *la ventana*
not far from the spring called: *el gallo.*

i wanted to keep us in
the long dream we planned.
you answered another call instead
and headed toward a mythical
watering place--   away from me.

i will follow the song
of blue mountain woman
and search for *hah pah nyi* sticks
to make *hutch a mun*
those prayer sticks that
make a proper connection.

i will make a bone whistle
to call on my ancestors.
it is important
that these things be done.

the sweet cedar smoke
cleans my memory
now/*huk ko*

restores the proper movement
the order of ritual things.

a ceremonial cycle begins
removes indecision and
scattered acts
restores control and direction
reminds me to keep harmony with
all living things.
oh srats/father sun
smiles.

the hot sweat bath
cleans my body
now/*huk ko*

prepares my being for
new journeys into
my life.

i move toward
the oak/*hah pah nyi* stands
at the edge of the black
malpais

that going down place-
to gather what i
left behind.

i sprinkle white
corn meal   to the
six directions
now/*huk ko*
and make my prayer
for moving
on again.

coral woman's song

she looked just like her
daughter-in-law
and i wondered who they were
some other time
while he mixed alarm clocks
and freeways for
revolutions in the mind.

this isn't concrete
they sd.
but nothing follows
when you refuse to agree.

the idea of concreteness
is as illusive as the
obsession that demands
its existence.

circle dancers
among the *wi ots*
once stomped the earth
back into place
because it tilted away from the sun.
i circle danced
with a mediterranean tribe
in stockton-
stomping that moment into place
to coincide with: twenty years
of memories dispersed and scattered
(returned to dust
coated with asphalt

linked with clocks and free ways
documented in my abstract mind.
and they presume
to tell me
-i- must build my **FREE**ways

with perceivable stuff
limited to their range
of perception

and i say:
catch me if you can.

squash blossoms

we chase dawn into sleep
alter days to fit within tendrils of smoke;
those fragile trails from dying embers.
what fuel is left to encourage
one last spark into flame?

parchment curls in smoke filled rooms behind
velvet draperies pulled shut.
what spark is left to rekindle
and birth once more?

you spoke of the wolf- lean and close
who knew hunger inside his ribbed coat alone.
i watch greyed countenances wince with recall,
not able to forget firelight fantasies
returning dreams to ashes mixed in sand.

i hear you   out of yesteryears
run back to those places called: used
to be.   another time.   another place.

cold despair in soft cushions of dark thought
walks the night through honky tonk bars
stalks neon glow into oblivion
spills lives into various gutters along the way.
the stench of desolation numbs the senses of
the most hardened street cleaners.

fog drifts descend warm and wet to moisten
evening winter streets.

blow the winds of hurricanes through the eye
of the universe when you exhale living breath.

the alchemists sought only special material
the sacred fabric of cells transmuted.
the dream is still there

enclosed in fact and fiction and i feel it
surge through your fingertips when
your hands cup my breasts
and the spark rushes down to ignite the
embers between my thighs
into flames.

vision: prophecy: ceremony:

these histories come together to dream a
time of never waiting and discover
the sound of minutes rushing.

morning clatters into inevitability
straightens itself here and there
then puzzles its way forward into mid-day
and finally early evening.
the heat, or lack of it presents
brief discomforts to the inhabitants of
the day.

the edge of illumination
clings perilously close to my thoughts
with remorse hidden among bits of
conversations and idle looks.

this clever path of attainment
solves itself with carefully
placed signposts (in odd places
obviously intent on keeping the
adherents focused toward
the proper events.

discourse pertaining to various
modes of travel rise and fall in
context quite naturally -no single
course of action defined more
outstanding than the other.

a momentum of speech and movement
clarifies the points of progress and
contributes to an ultimate understanding
of the complexities outlined
within the whole.

internal alignments continue to take place
appropriately within the framework designed
for the entire operation.

we rest on perilous heights
contained in visions long accumulated
and instruct those younger
hoping that the human circuitry
will have changed enough to
bypass ancient repetitions.

and though multiple examples lie in wait
on every bookshelf among the
histories invented
these human systems **will** re-enact the
countless versions of each event
until old age claims wisdom and
stars beckon thoughts of
alternative orders of being.

any present time will rise to greet
creative change.
barring that-   will wait around
for total acceptance
and if dismissed
will re-emerge   demanding notice
exclaiming all the while
the symbols built by
thoughtful beings.

afterwords: the artist as universe

> "the idea of concreteness
> is as illusive as the
> obsession that demands
> its existence."

Like the "damned quantum jumpiness" which so enraged Einstein, Carol Lee records/is a record of events as they are experienced — subjective transmutes into general, general into particular, particular into personal, without moving through any intervening space. Her body becomes any woman's body, becomes Woman's body, becomes any human's body, becomes any animal body, becomes landscape, becomes primal wind/mountain/ water/blood/bone/breath, becomes her body — the same particle/event-cluster perceived at different energy levels.

> "linked with clocks and freeways
> documented in my abstract mind-
> and they presume
> to tell me
> -***i***- must build my **FREE**ways
> with perceivable stuff
> limited to their range
> of perception"

Carol Lee is a poet, a painter, a cloth sculptor, a teacher, an administrator, a student, a computer operator, a woman, a mother, a daughter, a private, a general, a staff sergeant, a grandmother, an aunt, a dancer, a musician, an ecstatic, a depressive, a solid anchor, an emotional wreck, a descendant, an ancestor, an opinionated bitch, someone in a distant past, someone in a distant future, someone in a distant present, maiden, lover, hag, prophet, archeologist, logician, intuitive. . . and probably a lot of other things — but I've only known her for about thirteen years. Even if I have identified a number of her possible energy states, I have yet to identify the fundamental particle. She may be an oblique sense of humor.

> "we should remember that that *c'ko'yo* magic
> is still there
> working at the bottom of things
> and *tsush ki* will have the last laugh"

Perhaps she is an experiment in consciousness. Back before Whatever-the-hell-is-going-on-here got itself divided up into Philosophy, Religion, Science, History, Entertainment, and Advertising, Carol Lee was probably a lot more common. In this sense, she not only has but is our undivided attention. From any one viewpoint, it is at times difficult to determine whether or not the various people quoted, talked to, and/or talked about in her poems are separate entities or are parts or energy levels of Carol Lee herself.

> "occasionally - her memories coincided with a
> particular day   and a forgotten friend
> came to call. . .
>
> and the messages she sent herself
> moved her into other dreams."

If academic lecturers cannot accept her as a "real Indian" because she has been contaminated by other influences, then neither can she be accepted as a "real Lebneni", a "real European", a "real Scot", a "real American". If this line of argument is true, then no human being is a "real" anything once contaminated by contact with other "human beings". Perhaps this is Carol Lee's true audience — all those human beings who have had contact with other human beings.

This is the core of the problem faced in writing this "Afterword" to this collection of Carol Lee's works. Carol Lee wrote these poems out of her own experience, but I have been in and out of that experience for more than a dozen years. I have lived with some of these poems as a part of my experience for many of those years. They have entered my life, become part of my personal mythology. If I identified with parts of them then, can I un-identify with them now. An author creates a work, the work is perceived by others, what is perceived becomes part of the life experience of these others, one of these others becomes an author, an author creates a work . . . A person drowns . . . whose life passes before whose eyes? Whether this is a core Ontological/Epistemological/Etiological problem, or merely another aspect to be enjoyed depends on how it bothers you.

In the deserts of the Southwest, where Carol Lee grew up, there are mesas carved in volcanic ash. By day, people have walked on these mesas and on the saddleridges connecting them. On moonless nights, even the incredible blaze of desert stars is not enough to light these ways for walking. Yet — the paths carved by feet in daylight have powdered the ash of some of these trails in such a way that, on moonless nights, the paths catch the starlight and mix these diverse lights into a ghostly luminescence. You cannot read by this light, but it is quite bright enough for you to walk these paths safely. The many voices mingle here: ancient volcanoes, millenia of wind and water, centuries of people passing, moonless night, a myriad of myriads of stars, a magic path of ghostly luminescence, and someone to walk the path. One or more of these is Carol Lee — one or more of these is her poetry. And you, the reader, are one or more of these.

She says:

> "when i am finished   i will know the meanings of
>   my icons   and where
>   i have hidden them."

She answers:

> "and i say:
> catch me if you can."

D. Druid Spechtold
San Francisco
March, 1985

the author's story

because of Elias Lee Francis and Ethel Gunn Gottlieb, i am. my father was born in the spanish land grant town of seboyeta and my mother was born in laguna village. i was born in albuquerque, came home to paguate village on the laguna reservation, and later moved to the tiny town of cubero on the cubero land grant with my parents, when i was four. as daughter, grandaughter, and great grandaughter of indigenous american indian women from laguna pueblo and immigrant scotch and french men—on my mother's side—and immigrant lebanese pioneers—on my father's side—i am the product of two races and four distinct cultures. my european/middle eastern ancestors settled in new mexico territory in the late 1800's, in an area that once belonged to the laguna and acoma pueblo indians. my immediate as well as my extended family is as large and diverse as 'la tierra' of my birth and gave me an incredibly rich bi-racial, religious, political and multilingual heritage. I grew in the country, wild and free; rocks, trees, horses, sheep, cattle and southwestern ways, my childhood and teen-age reality. 'mi tierra encantada', along with this marvelous lineage and heritage deserve much of the credit for this collection of poems. this background is the foundation of my creative impetus and fundamentally, why i write as i do. additional credit is due my sisters and brothers, Kathleen Ann Swanquist, Paula Gunn Allen, E. Lee Francis III and John Cecil Francis, for they were my only playmates for many years as well as my closest friends and confidants. each of them are artists of suburb talent in their own right and their influence throughout my life is immeasurable. in 1966, i left new mexico with my two older children, Paul Frederick and Suecarol Bartolucci, leaving my family and a couple of ex-husbands behind, to 'be' part of the art scene that was flourishing in san francisco's north beach. Miguél Ráshid Sanchez, my youngest, was born in september of that year and by 1968, i was totally involved in the bay area arts community. over the last ten years, i have been bay area coordinator and then statewide director of the california poets in the schools program, appeared on pbs tv reading my poetry, then a writer in residence, shown my paintings and works in canvas, taught ethnic studies and women's studies courses at san francisco state university, american indian history and culture at the san francisco art institute and mills college, and travelled around the u.s. reading my poetry and giving lectures on cross-cultural curriculum- - writers and artists of color - american indian arts and artists. collections of my poems, *conversations from the nightmare*, (casa editorial) and *message bringer woman*, (taurean horn press) were published in 1975 and 1977.

i would like to acknowledge and thank Bill Vartnaw for his patient work on this manuscript and writing the introduction; Druid Spechtold for writing 'the artist as universe: afterwords', and years of friendship; and Thomas Allen for his loving patience and care and the photograph he provided for the back cover. Most of all, I would like to thank my parents for being who they are and continuously providing love and encouragement - no matter what i do or don't do.

june 21, 1985
santa margarita, california